THE INTENDERS HANDBOOK

A Guide to
The Intention Process
and
The Conscious Community
Revised 2007 Edition

Tony Burroughs

Dolphin Press

The Intenders Handbook

Copyright © 1997 by Tony Burroughs
All Rights Reserved
Printed in the United States of America
First Printing: November 1997
Sixth Printing: March 2007
ISBN: 0-9654288-1-8
Intenders Logo by Aquila Purpura

This book is dedicated to Mark, Tina, Betsy and you

*My sincere thanks to some very special Intenders:
Connie, Aaron, Karen, Lois, Alice, Alva, Spirit, Mark,
LouAnn, Erna, Kamele, Jeff, Pomaika'i, Loren, Kevin,
Kate, Jennifer, Patrice, Daniel, Mark, Jeri, Dian, Chris,
Garth, Dayadevi, Conrad, David, Thalia, Theo, Estelle,
Sharry, Susie, Sandy, Claudia, Walter, Darshan, Ajanel,
Donna Jo, Carolee, Bill, Shirley, Pattie, Teresa, Melissa,
Judi, Nathan, Mauricio, Ginny, Lisa, Jody, Sarito, Janice,
Ana Lia, Tim, Victoria, Arthor, Auriel, Vicki, Lee Ching,
and my beautiful sister in Spirit, Adrian Ulrey.*

All of the information and personal accounts
herein are based on true events

The Intenders of the Highest Good
Phone: (888) 422-2420
E-mail: office@intenders.com
Visit our website at: **www.intenders.com**

Published by Dolphin Press,
137 Kuakolu Place, Hilo, HI USA 96720

Table of Contents

PART I
SHARING YOUR DREAMS

Introduction

The Intenders of the Highest Good has always been a casual group. From the very beginning, we never made any rules or charged any dues. We didn't have a membership for people to join and there weren't any positions of leadership to fill. We came together in friendship, with an earnest desire to help each other. We wanted to be happy and to find a way to make our lives more fulfilled.

The old values and beliefs that we'd grown up with weren't working for us anymore. We were spending far too much of our time and energy spinning our wheels, doing things that brought us little or no lasting satisfaction.

The Intention Process and the Intenders Circles were created because we needed to learn a new way to manifest things. We wanted to do something that really worked.

You can create a world
that always supports you

The Mighty Manifesters

The purpose of this handbook is to help you make your life better. The Intenders of the Highest Good will show you how to make your dreams come true easily and with the least amount of effort. We've been practicing the ideas that are given in this handbook for several years and have found that the laws of manifestation work very efficiently for us when we do two simple things:

1. We say our intentions out loud everyday;
2. We meet together with like-minded friends in an Intenders Circle once a week.

This is all that needs to be done for us to start getting everything that we desire out of life. We must be willing to take a few moments away from our busy routines for these two important things (or something similar that may be called by another name) so that we can *consciously* turn our deepest desires into real-life experiences. Otherwise, we will remain unempowered and at the mercy of the ever changing world we live in.

To the men and women who can manifest whatever is needed in their lives, it doesn't matter how scarce things appear to be or what the newspapers and TV are saying. Self-empowered people simply observe the day-to-day challenges that are going on all around them, while manifesting a world of their own choosing - a world of peace and comfort. They live happily because that's what they've *intended* to do.

Reference Points

From the beginning of the Intenders, we have been guided by three reference points. A reference point for us is something that we know we can count on. The courageous mariners of old knew all about using points of reference. They would pick out certain stars, or a spot on the distant shoreline, and they would refer to these points when they wanted to know where they were and where they were going. Likewise, we Intenders also want to know where we are going in our lives.

Our three main points of reference are:

1. Our desires are in us to be fulfilled;

2. Our thoughts create our world; and

3. Our intentions must serve the highest and best good of the Universe, as well as the highest and best good of ourselves and others.

We have practiced these principles in our daily lives and in our Weekly Intenders Circles over the past several years and we know that they consistently produce the results that we are seeking.

*"The Intenders are on the fast track! We don't dwell on the dramas. We transmute them by going directly to the positive side of every issue and **intending** exactly how we desire things to come out.*

"We share our dreams, instead of our dramas."

Philip Moore

Our Desires Are In Us To Be Fulfilled

We are here to live fully and freely. Our lives are to be enjoyed. We did not come to this beautiful, abundant Earth to suffer and go without all of the good things that life has to offer. Our desires are in us to be fulfilled - and they can be fulfilled with a minimum of effort by using the laws of direct manifestation.

The Intenders know that there is plenty of everything for everybody. There's an abundance of resources, enjoyable work to do, tools, toys, recreational opportunities, relationships, and so forth. It's time for all of us to stop creating scarcity and start learning how we can bring our dreams into physical reality.

The Intenders of the Highest Good use an easy and fun method that we call the Intention Process. By practicing it for a short time everyday, and by going to a Weekly Intenders Circle, you will be putting the laws of direct manifestation to work for you. And very soon, sometimes spontaneously, your desires will be fulfilled and your lifelong dreams will come true.

Your desires come from that which moves you forward

"When I arrived at my first Intenders Circle, I was homeless. I'd been trying to find a way to scrape up enough money to rent a small place, but things just weren't working out for me. I was getting desperate!

"My friends who took me to the Intenders Circle told me not to hold back. They said that, at an Intenders Circle, 'the sky's the limit,' and that I should ask for my heart's desire. I made an intention to find a place of my own where I would be very, very happy - and I asked that it come to me freely and easily.

"It wasn't two days later and a lady who had been at the meeting called me and said she was going abroad for at least three years. She'd thought about selling her house, but it was such a lovely custom home, right down by the beach, that she couldn't bring herself to part with it. Maybe she'd be back someday, but, in the meantime, would I be interested in caretaking it for free?"

Karen Reid

~ ~ ~

What you are reaching toward
is also reaching out toward you

Our Thoughts Create Our World

There are a lot of different ways to say it: our thoughts create our experiences; our thoughts create our reality; our thoughts create our future; our thoughts create our world. Any way you look at it, our thoughts are creating **everything**!

"We realized that we needed to make the best use of our thoughts. We needed to bring focus to our thoughts and give our lives a positive direction. That's when we stumbled across the word 'intention.' Sally heard it in a dream and we looked it up later in the dictionary. It said that 'intention' was a 'moving toward.' So we realized we'd found a way to actually start moving toward something by thinking about it and intending it."
Mariel Moore

Every thought that we think is getting ready to manifest. The more attention we give to it, the more it moves toward the surface of our experience. This is the way things work, and still, quite frequently, we unconsciously entertain conflicting thoughts. For example, we make our daily intentions early in the morning, and then, a couple of hours later, we're allowing ourselves to dwell on all sorts of other thoughts that are telling us that our intentions couldn't possibly come true.

Perhaps, early in the morning, we'll intend to get a musical instrument and intend to learn how to play it. Everything goes along fine and we're trusting in the Intention Process until sometime around noon when a persuasive voice comes into our head and says that we can't afford a musical instrument right now; or, we don't really have a good ear for music; or, we're getting too old to learn how to play an instrument, and so forth. The voice continues on and on, and the negative doubts and worries begin to interfere with the manifestation of our original, positive intention.

The Intenders of the Highest Good are steadily raising our level of consciousness by keeping a closer watch on all of our thoughts. We're learning to tame the negative thoughts and take our own power back. We're *choosing* which thoughts we desire to put our attention on by envisioning only positive outcomes and turning the undesired thoughts around in mid-air, before they gain momentum.

For many of us, the key to getting rid of these negative doubts and worries - and their accompanying undesired experiences - is to keep our lives full. We make our intentions early in the morning, and then we go about the rest of our day enjoying ourselves and doing the things that we like to do: baking goodies, surfing interesting sites on the net (**www.intenders. com**), puttering in the yard, playing music, etc. Then, if an undesired thought comes in, we recognize it, bless it, send it back where it came from, and we go back to our baking, websurfing, gardening, or music-making - knowing, without a doubt, that our early morning's intention is on its way to us. We are light-hearted and divinely nonchalant, having as much fun as we can, while remaining open and ready to receive.

※ ※ ※

Pizza

Here is an excerpt from Chapter 10 of
THE INTENDERS OF THE HIGHEST GOOD

They all laughed, and Philip resumed the conversation.

"I'll give you another example, Liz.

"Suppose you go into a pizza parlor and order your pizza at the counter. They give you a cold drink, point you toward a red-colored table, and tell you that your pizza will be ready in twenty minutes.

"You go sit down and wait. While you're waiting, you do not ponder and worry about whether they'll get the pizza right. You've ordered mushrooms, bell peppers and extra cheese. You don't concern yourself with the possibility that maybe they'll accidentally put on

some black olives or onions. You don't worry that they might burn the crust, or, worse yet, put on some of those nasty anchovies that make you so sick to your stomach. You just trust that the lady who took your order will make sure it's correct. If there is some problem, the pizza lady will take it back and have it fixed according to your exact instructions. The pizza place wants you to be happy. They're not out to get you. They want you to keep coming back for more.

"Likewise, the Universe desires to be our friend. It is we who sit and dwell on anchovies and burnt crust. We bring these undesired things to ourselves. Remember, we said that what we think creates our experiences. And so, if we worry about worst-case scenarios, those things tend to come to us. It is not a wise idea to draw unhappy, stressful experiences into our lives, but that is surely what we do when we get to worrying about things.

"If we concentrate our thoughts on problems, that's what we'll get. Or, if we concentrate our thoughts on beneficence, that's what we'll get. Whatever it is that we concentrate our thoughts on, <u>that's what we'll get.</u>

"So, we can change our attitudes. Instead of envisioning burnt crust and anchovies, we can think of the best pizza we ever tasted while we wait.

"Sounds good, doesn't it?"

~ ~ ~

The Intention Process

The Intention Process is just about as simple as it can be. All you have to do is say **"I intend"** and then follow it up with whatever it is that you desire. It could be anything! You could intend to have a new coat for yourself or you could intend for world peace. Since there are no limits on what you can think about, there are no limits on what you can intend!

*For me, I get up every morning and **I intend** that I am joyful and happy. **I intend** fun and laughter. **I intend** that I am in perfect health - rejuvenated, aligned, balanced, and feeling physically great all of the time. **I intend** that I am always guided, guarded, and protected. These are a few of the general intentions that I start with everyday and then I look around at my life to see what I am needing. If the old wheelbarrow just broke, **I'd intend** that I have a new one. If the computer decided to go on the fritz, **I'd intend** that it gets fixed. I don't leave anything out because there's no reason to hold back!*

*I like to make a few intentions each day about my personal traits. Sometimes **I intend** that I am a more compassionate person; or **I intend** that I'm more kind or gentle. And sometimes, especially when there are a lot of dramas going on all around me, **I intend** that I* *see everyone in their highest light and every event from its highest point of view. That way, I'm able to observe all of the sorrow and suffering in the world and still remain uplifted. **I intend** that I remember that it doesn't do anybody any good to drop down into someone else's challenges and become troubled or sad along with them. It's much better to set an example by staying happy and cheerful.*

*After intending for things like this for awhile, I take a closer look at the world at large and make a few intentions for it too. For example, **I intend** that men, women, and children everywhere experience grace. And **I intend** that peace and harmony blossom all across the land. And **I intend** that this Earth is living in its highest light, and that, within our environment, the air we breathe is clean and crisp; the water everywhere is crystal clear and delicious; the soil is abundant with lush growth and beautiful fruit is dripping from the trees; the animals are honored and respected; and people all over the world are happy and smiling because they're being given everything that they need!*

*And, last but not least, **I intend** that all of my thoughts, words, and deeds serve the highest and best good of the Universe, myself, and everyone everywhere.*

So be it and so it is!

Tony Burroughs

Picture the end result from the beginning

What You Say Is What You Get

After we'd been doing our intentions for awhile, we realized how important clarity is. How we use our words really <u>does</u> matter! The more exact we become with our words when we make our intentions, the easier it is to manifest exactly what we desire. If we are vague or unclear with our words, the circuits seem to get jumbled and things don't always work out.

"I remember when I learned about clarity. Last year, when I didn't have much money and my old tennis shoes were falling apart, I went to the Sunday Intenders Circle and put an intention into the circle to manifest a new pair of shoes. I didn't have the slightest idea how I was going to get them. I just trusted that they would come to me.

"Now . . . I must tell you that I'm a bit of a scavenger and I keep my eyes open for treasures all the time. And sure enough, on the Tuesday after the circle, we were dropping some rubbish off at the dump and, sitting there on the ledge, right beside the chute, was an almost brand new pair of fancy running shoes. They were just what I wanted! I happily tossed them into the back seat, but when I got home and tried them on, they didn't fit.

"They were a size 8 - and I wear a 10.

"I had easily manifested a new pair of shoes, but I had neglected to tell the Universe that I wanted them to fit me. From that day on, I got real clear with all of my intentions. And three days later, after giving the size 8s away, a buddy of mine gave me a beautiful pair of pumpup basketball shoes - size 10."

Rob Eastman

So much of our lives have been spent thinking that we can be frivolous with our spoken words, but now we're finding out that it's to our great advantage to be clear and concise about what we desire to manifest. We know that our words are the building-blocks of our future.

The spoken word is a very important part of what the Intenders do. It isn't a necessity to speak our intentions out loud, but there are several benefits in doing so. Saying our intentions out loud is making an announcement to the Universe; it tells the Universe, with no uncertainty, that this is what we desire to manifest. Our clarity is enhanced by speaking our words boldly to the Universe. Also, we learn more about ourselves when we listen to our own intentions being said aloud. When we say our intentions silently, we tend to skip over items that we might pay more attention to if we were to say them out loud.

Our vocabulary has even started to change as a result of our pursuit of clarity. We've eliminated five words that kept us unempowered and no longer serve us well. In our circles, we've stopped using *trying, hoping, wanting, to be,* and *not* because they were interfering with the manifestation of our intentions. We eliminated *"trying"* because it's a halfway word. It provides a built-in excuse to be unsuccessful. If you're having a conversation with someone and you say, "I'll meet you tomorrow morning at 11 o'clock," and their response is, "I'll *try,*" it isn't very reassuring.

We've also dropped *"hoping"* from our vocabulary. When a person is *"hoping"* that something will happen, he or she is holding on to a little bit of doubt about whether their intention will really come true. If they replace *"I hope"* with **"I intend"**, and really trust in the Intention Process, then things will begin to change for them. They will stop limiting themselves unknowingly.

Wanting is another word that we refrain from using in our Intenders Circles because it implies that there is a scarcity of things. We looked it up in the dictionary and it said that if we were in a state of *wanting*, then we were lacking. So now, instead of saying, "I *want* a new car," we say, **"I intend** that I have a new car." This slight change, though very subtle, has taken scarcity out of the picture and brought us much closer to our own empowerment.

Another phrase we've recently gotten rid of is *"to be."* In our circles, we say, "I intend that I am happy," for instance, instead of saying, "I intend *to be* happy." This small but very important change has produced extremely rewarding results for us. It brings everything into the present time, as opposed to keeping our desires somewhere off in the future. There is a big difference in intending *to be* happy and intending that you are happy now. By intending that you are happy now, you are seeing the end result from the beginning. Otherwise, you can intend *to be* happy and the Universe may follow your exact instructions and keep you in a state of readiness for a very long time, waiting *to be* happy. If you don't rephrase your intentions, you could easily remain on the brink of your happiness indefinitely without ever quite reaching it.

When you first begin to form your intentions into words, it's always best to take a moment and create a very clear picture in your mind of that which you truly desire to manifest. See yourself in the picture *acting as if* it has already happened. Then you can use the words "I intend that I am _____" and know that you've gotten off to an excellent start with your intentions.

Sometimes it also helps to imagine that you are working hand in hand with your guides, helpers, or angels from other realms, and that these helpers are there to serve you. They listen closely to your intentions and go scurrying throughout the far corners of the Universe, taking the thoughts and words that you have provided and then delivering them back to you down here on Earth in the forms and substances that you call third-dimensional experience. When you state your intentions in the present and envision them as if they have already occurred, you send the clearest possible message out to your helpers. You've made their job a lot easier, while optimizing your own potential for bringing your dreams into physical reality.

The last word we've eliminated is "*not*." Our guides told us that our subconscious mind is unable to recognize the word "*not*" and that things would work out much better for us if we put our intentions out to the Universe in a positive way. For example, instead of saying, "I intend that I am *not* sick anymore", now we would say, "I intend that I am always in excellent health."

By saying things in a positive way, our entire lives are becoming more positive. We are subtly empowering ourselves by getting rid of the negatives in our speech. And we're becoming more aware when those around us are unempowered. You can easily tell what's going on in the lives of your friends and acquaintances by listening closely to what they're saying. If they are using these unempowered words, then they are most-likely creating scarcity and limitation in their lives. You can help them to raise their level of consciousness by setting an example for them and, when they're receptive, by gently explaining to them how their words are limiting their experience. When you do this, everyone is uplifted. And that upliftment radiates outward into your community and into the world you live in.

The source of your supply is so immense.
It's all there for you
just waiting for you to tap into it

The Intenders Circle

Since the beginning of humankind, we have come together in circles. We've sat around campfires, steaming rocks, food, drummers, and displays of entertainment. Even the meetings of wise elders were often held in circles. In a circle, everyone can easily see and hear everyone else. The circle puts everyone at ease, on an equal standing. And it allows each person to freely contribute to the whole group.

We started out with four of us sitting around a table on the patio once a week. We'd go around the circle and each of us would say our gratitudes and then our intentions for the things that we desired to manifest in our lives. Pretty soon, we were getting phenomenal results, a bunch of our friends had joined us, and the feeling of being part of a family had awakened in all of us. As the group got larger and larger, we began listening to each other even more closely. We became cheerleaders for each other, really being happy for someone else when their intentions came to life.

We also discovered a lot of joy in keeping a watchful eye out for the things that others in our circle had intended to manifest. Bartering, trading, and sharing became commonplace, and we felt a new strength now that we were part of a network where everyone was helping everyone else. The Intention Process was working and our lives changed quickly for the better!

"I always had a knack for working on computers. When my friends would raise their hands in the air and threaten to bash their computers, I would offer to fix them. I'd been teaching part-time in the evenings, but I really wanted to be working full-time fixing computers. I also had a desire to be able to make lowcost secondhand or rebuilt computers available to the people in the area. The only problem I had was getting parts. I wasn't in a big city where parts were easy to find.

"About that time, I happened to go to an Intenders Circle. That night I made an intention to leave my teaching position and somehow, some way, start my own business fixing and rebuilding computers.

"Four days later, a friend of mine told me about a place where I could put a bid in on a whole container-load of good computer parts - CPUs, keyboards, printers, everything, including the monitors! I got the bid and, within two weeks, I rented a wonderful warehouse in town and stacked it full of all kinds of computer equipment. Everything I'd intended to have was right there at my fingertips!

"Before I knew it, people were lined up at my door needing help with their computers. And when I'd help them, I couldn't resist also telling them about the Intenders."

Aaron Christensson

~ ~ ~

"There really is power in an Intenders Circle! My car threw a rod last summer when I was in between jobs. I made an intention to have another car come to me free, since I didn't have any extra money at the time. Four days later, my son called me up and, before I could say anything, asked me if I knew anybody who wanted a car - a nice, older, but sporty VW. He said that it was taking up too much space beside his carport, but that it ran great. And, it was first come, first serve.

"Within an hour, I caught a ride to his place, started up the car, and drove it away.

"It felt like Christmas in July!"

Wayde Cameron

~ ~ ~

~ The Five Easy Steps ~

1. Test the Intention Process and Be Open
2. Get your first "win" and acknowledge that it works by expressing your gratitude
3. Develop your trust by practicing and getting more "wins"
4. Notice that your trust turns into a "knowing" that you can manifest anything you desire
5. Have fun, stay filled with gratitude, and always remember the Highest Good

Gratitude

Gratitude is what makes the Intention Process work. It's the acknowledgment that the intentions we've made in the past have come true. When we express our gratitude, we're saying "thank you" to the Universe for bringing us the things that we've asked for. We're saying that we recognize that a connection exists between ourselves and the Universe, that we appreciate this connection, and know that we can call on it at any time.

There is always a lot of gratitude expressed in our Intenders Circles. In fact, that's what our Intenders Circles are for - to make our intentions and to express our gratitude for their manifestation.

When an Intender speaks of gratitude, it shows everyone in the circle that the laws of manifestation work. It gives those who still carry doubts and skepticism a newfound confidence. It heightens their level of trust when they see their fellow Intenders "winning."

And that's how it all starts. We make an intention, and soon, when it has manifested, we feel like we've gotten a "win" - and we say so by stating our gratitude. The Intention Process has come full circle. It started out with an intention and it ended with a statement of gratitude.

Once we've seen ourselves and our friends get a "win" or two, it gets much easier for all of us. We put even more trust in the Intention Process and then we get more and more "wins." Pretty soon, we're "winning" all of the time! Eventually, we'll look around us and see that the world we're living in is the one we've intended for ourselves. We will have created *everything* in our world consciously. When enough of us have done this, others will learn from our example, and we will all begin to walk this Earth free and full of gratitude.

"Last Spring, during the potluck at an Intenders meeting, a very successful woman was telling us about how she manifests things. She was using money as an example. She said that she was grateful for it, both before and after it arrives. That got me started thinking.

"Up until then, money was always a challenge for me. Every time a bill would come in the mail, I would get upset. Right away, I would start to complain and I'd walk around muttering and wondering how I was ever going to pay it.

"But since that meeting, I've started doing something different. Now, I thank the Universe when I get a bill in the mail. I think of all the wonderful things that the bills are providing for me and I'm really grateful for them.

"Needless to say, everything is much better financially for me now. Since I've started being grateful, I've received more money than I ever had before. It just keeps flowing in, like water from the kitchen faucet. Sometimes I'm even pleasantly surprised by where it comes from!"

Ron Merriweather

The World's Best Insurance Policy

We always say that in order for our intentions to manifest that they must serve the highest and best good of the Universe and the highest and best good for ourselves and others. Anytime we gather together in an Intenders Circle it is understood that all of our intentions serve the highest good, *but it's a good idea to say it anyway!*

On occasion, we've had people who wanted to make an intention but didn't care whether it served the highest and best good or not. They just wanted their desire to come to them, no matter what. And guess what happened? It did. You can manifest your intentions whether you ask that they serve the highest and best good or not. It's just that you could easily find yourself in an odd or uncomfortable predicament after your intention comes to you. Sometimes you'll even wish you hadn't made the intention in the first place.

'It seems like every so often I have to learn my lessons the hard way. I'd been coming to the Intenders for several weeks and everything was clicking just right for me. I had a new, loving relationship and a wonderful place to live. The only loose end I had in my life was that my credit cards were extended to their limits, and I needed a part-time job. The bills were piling up and the creditors were calling me almost everyday.

I needed some work badly, and I didn't care how I got it. All I wanted was for the creditors to leave me alone.

"So I went out and applied for several jobs and found one that I really hoped I would get. It involved taking care of a very nice elderly lady in her home, right near where I lived. I wouldn't even have to get in my car in the mornings. I could jog to work. It seemed like the perfect job, and it paid more than any of the others. I didn't want to take any chances.

"That night, when I put my intention into the Intenders Circle, I didn't say the part about the highest and best good on purpose. Sally asked me about it and I said that this job was just too important. I wanted it at any cost, regardless of whether it was for my highest good or for anybody else's. I remember looking around me and seeing several of my friends in the circle shaking their heads.

"Well, everything happened so quickly. I got the job, but, within a week, I found that I wasn't strong enough to lift the lady and take care of her properly. I pulled a muscle in my back and every time I would help her out of bed, it would hurt us both. Things steadily went from bad to worse. After a few more days, I quit.

"And, as if that wasn't enough, later on, I found out that there had been another stronger, more qualified person who'd applied for the job at the same time I did. That person really needed the work too, but was passed over and was forced to move away because of me.

"I felt terrible.

"Now I never forget to ask that all of my intentions are for the highest and best good for everyone concerned."

Patti Revardo

Occasionally an Intender will have been putting the same intention into the circle week after week with no results. They have a desire so strong that it has crystallized in them, and yet it just won't seem to manifest. This is when we say that the highest and best good clause has kicked in. It's simply not in the highest and best interests of the person for that particular desire to materialize.

This always presents the Intender with a very interesting decision. They've had so many of their intentions come true, therefore they know that the Intention Process works. At the same time, they also know that they wouldn't want something to manifest if it wasn't for their own highest good.

After a great deal of soul-searching, most often they'll let the desire go - and, in this way, they are steadily bringing themselves into closer alignment with the highest good.

"When we first started to use the Intention Process, we thought that the only thing we were doing was learning how to manifest things so we'd be happier. It wasn't until we'd been at it for well over a year that we realized something else was happening. Not only were

our dreams coming true, but we were also letting go of old stuff that we'd been hanging onto forever. It was that old stuff that was holding us back from living in our highest light.

"On one hand, our desires were being fulfilled; and, on the other hand, we were giving up our old desires that hadn't manifested. Pretty soon, we noticed that we didn't have as many desires as before. They had all either been manifested or let go of.

"That's when things started getting really good! We began to feel lighter and freer. The Intention Process was lining us up with our highest good, and what was being brought to us was a more wonderful, much grander gift than we had received from the small, mundane intentions that we had manifested since we first started. It was as if we were sprouting wings."

Sally Moore

Toning: The Sound of Oneness

We always end our Intention Circles with a toning. We've learned that something very special happens when people tone together. A Oneness occurs. You can feel it, and it feels good. Your Spirit lights up. You're uplifted. And all you have to do is make a sound.

The toning that we follow our Intenders Circle with is one of the highlights of the whole week for many of us. And it's so easy. In fact, it's probably the easiest way for a community of people to experience a Oneness.

Over the years, we've experimented with a lot of different toning methods and most of them work just fine. You can use any approach that you want, as long as you end up in the Oneness.

Here's how we do it: after everyone's intentions are put into the circle, we'll stand up and hold hands. Someone will make *an announcement* that we see all of our intentions going out to the Universe so that they will return to us in great abundance. At this time we also call upon our Spiritual guides, angels, helpers, and all those who stand with us in dedicating our intentions to the highest and best good. Oftentimes, before we do our toning, we'll call them by name to join our circle. (Not all of the Intenders Circles in our area choose to call upon their spiritual helpers, but our circle wouldn't think of toning without them.)

A typical pre-toning announcement that we have used in our Intenders Circles

"We take all of the intentions made here tonight and we send them out to the Universe on a pillar of white light that we create right here in this circle. We envision this pillar of light going up through the roof of this house and reaching out into the heavens above for as far as we can imagine . . . and now we see it going through the floor beneath us, connecting us to the heart of Mother Earth . . . and we see it expanding now, out past the

walls of this building and across the streets of this community and all across this land, inspiring and uplifting everyone it touches. And now we invite and invoke our guides and helpers. We call Mother Mary, Buddha, Jesus Christ, Lee Ching, Kuan Yin, St. Francis, Krishna, All Our Relations, The Ascended Masters, The Archangels, Moses, Mohammed, Yogananda, Gandhi, 'Abdu'l Baha, St. Germain, (add your favorite guides), and all those who stand for the <u>highest</u> good. We give great thanks that you join us here today and we ask that our intentions return to us in great measure. And, as always, we say that, in order to manifest, all of our intentions must serve the highest and best good of the Universe, ourselves and all others. So be it and so it is."

Then we pick a sound that feels comfortable for all of us, like Om, Aah, Home, Hah or God. When we tone we keep it going, as if we're singing a round. We've discovered that it's best if we tone for at least three or four minutes or until we reach the point when our sounds have joined together and we have achieved a Oneness.

After the toning is finished, we stand quietly for a few moments and bask in the Oneness. We've been ending our Intenders Circles this way for several years now and we know that it works. We know that the toning will take us into the Oneness - and we'll walk away feeling great!

***Lead yourself to harmony
and then let harmony take over from there***

All You Have To Do Is Ask

After the toning, we take a ten minute break. This time is spent snacking some more, socializing, and generally feeling good because of the effect of our toning together. Some people choose to leave at this point because they have to be home early. But those who stay are in for quite a treat.

This is when we have a special 30 minute spiritual guidance session. Someone will read an uplifting story, or we'll listen to a cassette tape that presents a higher point of view. Most of the time, however, we'll invite our Spiritual Guides in and they will come and talk to us. We have been blessed from the beginning of the Intenders to have some very special *messengers* in our group.

The Spiritual Guides that we have been listening to each week have helped everyone in our group immeasurably. Many of us were skeptical to begin with, but that didn't seem to matter. Our guides have proven themselves time and time again. They have given us strength and a feeling of being loved very deeply. They have answered all of our questions about the challenges we've been experiencing in our daily lives, always inspiring us to be all that we can be.

It's not necessary for every Intenders group to have a *messenger* (someone who is in contact with the angels and guides), but it sure helps when you can occasionally talk with someone who sees things from a

31

higher perspective. If you don't have someone who is a clear *messenger* in your group and you'd like one, all you have to do is ask. By putting a clear intention into your circle and dedicating it to the highest good, the Universe will bring the appropriate *messenger* to you.

"If you're interested in becoming a messenger, you'll want to learn to give yourself the proper instructions. What you say in your instructions or prayers before you start to channel will have a great deal to do with who shows up and what is said.

"These instructions are very important. Even if you're listening to another messenger and wondering whether the information is accurate, pay close attention to the words that they say before they begin. They must be willing to ask for the highest good or that their words come from the highest light. What you ask for is what you'll get.

"Here are the instructions that I use:

"I ask that everything needing to be known is known here today;

"I intend that we are all guided, guarded, and protected at all times;

"I intend that all of my words are clear, precise, uplifting, and helpful; and that they serve the highest and best good of the Universe, myself, and all beings everywhere.

"So be it and so it is."

Mariel Moore

PART II
HOW TO CREATE
YOUR OWN
INTENDERS CIRCLE

The Intenderpreneur

The Intenderpreneur is the person who takes it upon himself or herself to start a new Intenders Circle. These resourceful people make all the arrangements for having the first meeting of the Intenders in their area. They make the necessary phone calls and announcements so that anyone who might be interested in coming to an Intenders Circle has the opportunity to do so. The Intenderpreneur will find a comfortable location, preferably in a private home, to meet until a more permanent place can be established and agreed upon by the group. It's common for Intenders Circles to end up being held at the Intenderpreneur's home permanently.

At the meetings, the Intenderpreneur distributes copies of the format and newcomer information on pp. 40 &41, the gratitudes and intentions templates on pp. 70 & 71, and keeps track of all of the names, addresses and phone numbers of everyone who comes to the circles. S/he is also responsible for maintaining a smooth flow during the meetings. We've found that if we don't make a firm guideline about what time the potluck and the meditation start, then these things tend to start later and later. We think it's unfair for those who've come to the meeting on time to be kept waiting by others.

It's up to the Intenderpreneur to keep things moving so that the people who have a long way to go to get home aren't kept too late into the evening. The Intenderpreneur also sets the precedent for when personal announcements are to be made. During the potluck or during the break are appropriate times for people to talk about workshops, circulate flyers, or make announcements, rather than talking about these kinds of things during the Intenders Circle.

It's important to understand that the Intenderpreneur is not the leader of the group. The group belongs to itself. There are no appointed leaders. We think that every Intender is a leader and, therefore, any major decisions are made by all those who come to the meeting.

We are very grateful to the Intenderpreneurs for all the work that they do. Many people, friends and strangers alike, are touched by those who've had the insight to start an Intenders Circle.

"I intend that, from this moment forward, you and I and all of the people we come in contact with, and all of the people they come in contact with, and all of the people they contact - until it fills the entire Earth - live in utter joy and peace."

Betsy Palmer Whitney

The Conscious Community

In order for our dreams of a clean, peaceful, high-quality, living environment to come into reality, people must work together. Deep inside each of us, we know that a better world awaits us when we stop separating ourselves from one another. The competition in the marketplace, political standards, self-serving media scenarios, and so forth have continually worked to keep us apart from our fellowman, but have not brought us happiness in return.

Our grandparents still remember when neighbors were supporting each other and looking for ways to help one another. Everyone saw the value in each person and enjoyed unparalleled benefits from living together in harmony. The community spirit was alive and well.

Many people remember those happy times and long for a return to them. They're searching for a community that embodies a support system based on upliftment. They won't be satisfied to line themselves up with an inflexible dogma or any model that separates them from each other. They seek something higher.

Those who are actively working for a better world are now being intuitively guided to seek the company of others with high ideals. The messages of peace and love that surfaced in the 1960s are beginning to come back again - only this time, they're taking on a vastly different form. In the 60s, people lived in communes apart from society, renting big houses or moving out to the hills. In the near future, communities are not going to be based on how close people live to one another. People will live wherever they choose, but they will gather together periodically. These communities will consist of people who may even live at great distances from one another, but they will share a like-mindedness and a light-heartedness at a higher level of consciousness.

A weekly Intenders Circle is the perfect place for people to meet together with others who really stand for the highest good. There is a special quality about people who tell themselves that they are Intenders of the Highest Good. Others are attracted to them. They will be the leaders of the communities of the future because they will have already learned how to manifest a happy reality for themselves.

If you truly seek to add constructively to your world and be of service to yourself and others, now is the time for you to take every opportunity you can to be in a community environment. The Intenders of the Highest Good and many other similar groups are coming together all across the land. The people in these communities intend to live in a world of peace and are able to create it! Peace is prevailing on this Earth by our joining together and *intending it* into existence.

Peace is truly possible - **in our lifetime!**

~ ~ ~

The Extenders
of the
Highest Good

There are always Intenders and Intenderpreneurs who step forward with enthusiasm and desire to participate more than just once a week. Most often, these people share several things in common. They're natural networkers, looking to extend themselves out into their community and beyond. They're also holding onto a vision of how wonderful this world is when enough of us have come together for the highest good of all concerned. And they always delight in seeing the glow on the faces of newcomers who have just finished participating in their first Intention Circle.

The Extenders of the Highest Good is a core group made up of experienced Intenders from all of the nearby Intenders Circles. These "Extenders" are ready to help others learn the Intention Process and to help others set up new Intenders Circles of their own. The overall focus of the Extenders is to hold all things in the highest light, to educate newcomers, and to let people know when and where nearby weekly Intenders Circles are being held.

The inaugural get-together of the Extenders of the Highest Good took place because we realized that it is very helpful to have an experienced Intender come to the first few meetings of a new Intenders Circle. We knew that when an experienced Intender visits a new circle the format and the flow of the new circle are established much quicker, and many questions that might not have otherwise been answered are answered. The new circle is immediately empowered by the spark that the experienced Intender brings.

New Intenders are always inspired by the first-hand intention stories and the gratitude expressed by experienced Intenders. Even more than that, the experienced Intender is a catalyst. S/he carries a connection to all of the other Intenders Circles. Because of the Extender, new friendships are formed and many people who previously thought that they were working alone are pleasantly surprised to find themselves joined by others nearby who share the same high ideals and intentions. Our Spirit brightens as we are linked together with other lightworkers, all working for the highest good.

Extenders of the Highest Good Circles evolve on their own. As each geographical area blossoms with Intenders Circles, there will be several people who see the wisdom in uniting these circles together. A Solstice or Equinox Gathering is one of the best ways to do this. In Northern California, we held a Summer Solstice Gathering and, out of this, a core group of Extenders was created. Anyone who desired to take part in this core group wrote their name and phone number down on a sign-up sheet and, soon thereafter, we held the first meeting of the Extenders in that area.

Today, the Extenders of the Highest Good Circles are made up of high-spirited, conscious Intenders that all of the Intenders Circles in an area can call upon for help or guidance. These Extenders are able to explain the Intention Process clearly and show others what goes on in a typical Intention Circle. They also help new Intenders clarify their thoughts and words so that each person in the circle is able to manifest desired experiences right away. And they set an example - just by their presence, their gentle encouragement, and their stories of success - that inspires everyone who comes to the Intenders.

Involvement in an Extenders Circle is voluntary and, as with the individual Intenders Circles, participation is open to all who are genuinely interested. The Extenders get together for a potluck at least every three months, and there is a lot of networking done on the telephone and via e-mail in the interim.

Every community needs a core group to perpetuate itself, and it's important for the members of the core group to stay in close contact with one another. The people must be committed, responsible, and have an extraordinary respect for each other and for all life.

The original core group of the Intenders is still as strong in Spirit today as it was when we first met.

Much good comes to you
when you help each other

The Friendly Format

When the Intenders first started getting together, we experimented with many different formats and agendas. It was easy to tell which ones worked because we'd hear the expressions of gratitude right away. When something didn't work, we didn't hesitate to discard it immediately.

The 8-step format listed below is the one that we use in our Intenders Circles today. It is this unique format that has made the Intenders so successful. Thousands of people from all over the world have experienced profound results by following our friendly format. Whether you're a small circle of friends coming together for the first time, or you're an already established group of people who have been meeting regularly for years, we suggest that you test this format for yourselves.

Here are the format and information pages that we've been giving to newcomers to our circle. Feel free to copy them and pass them out at your meetings.

THE INTENDERS CIRCLE FORMAT

1. Blessing of food

2. Potluck

3. Short Guided Meditation

4. Explanation of THE INTENTION PROCESS to Newcomers

5. THE INTENTION CIRCLE

6. Toning

7. Break (more eating and socializing)

8. Spiritual Guidance Session

The Intenders Newcomer Information Sheet

- Our thoughts create our experiences
- Saying our *intentions* outloud focuses our thoughts
- There is power in the spoken word
- Positive thoughts bring positive experiences
- Negative thoughts bring undesired experiences
- It's important to trust and know that the things that we *intend* are coming to us because dwelling on doubts can interfere with the manifestation of our positive *intentions*
- We always ask that in order for our *intentions* to come to us, *they must serve the highest and best good of the Universe, ourselves, and all others*
- As we go around the circle, each person expresses their *gratitude* for the *intentions* that have manifested for them and then states their new *intentions*
- The power of the Intenders Circle arises from everyone supporting everyone else's *intentions*
- Clarity is important
- We eliminate such words as **trying, hoping, wanting, to be** and **not**
- We say things in a positive way: for example, instead of saying, "*I INTEND* that I am not afraid anymore," we would say, "*I INTEND* that I am courageous."
- We don't name sicknesses or diseases in our circles; we see everyone in their highest light
- We say our *intentions* daily, and we gather together in an Intenders Circle once a week
- We don't dwell on **how** or **when** our *intentions* will manifest for us; we just know that they will
- And we always end our *intentions* with our seven favorite words - **So be it and so it is !**

PART III
SHINING YOUR LIGHT

Fine-Tuning Our Words

There are many different ways to raise our level of consciousness. Consciousness is awareness and as we become more aware of the habitual words and word patterns that we and those around us are using, we can make great changes in our lives. By eliminating certain words that are no longer serving us from our daily expression, we cause new possibilities to open up before us. Our whole life brightens.

The Intenders of the Highest Good understand that the exactness of our words counts. We know, beyond all doubt, that the words we are using are constantly determining the kind of experiences we will have. By the same token, we have become more aware of when we are projecting an experience out into our world that we really, in our hearts, do not desire to see manifested. People do this unconsciously in their everyday conversation quite often. We call it negative projection or self-sabotage, and we gently point it out to each other when it happens in an Intenders Circle.

Much of the time, these self-sabotaging words and

phrases are added onto what we have just said, like an afterthought. For example, you'll frequently hear someone say, "I intend that the repairs go easily and effortlessly, *without too many problems.*" By adding on these last four words, they've suddenly undermined their original intention. They've sabotaged their own future by bringing "*problems*" into the picture.

When we Intenders catch ourselves projecting an undesired experience like this, we immediately remind ourselves of one of the main reference points in the Intention Process - that our thoughts and our words are constantly creating our world. The old saying, "As you believe, so it shall be for you" is a great truth. Since our words are exact reflections of what we believe, it is prudent for us to be much more careful with the words we are using. It's simply not in our highest and best interests to continue to be frivolous with our words. These words have power. They can either limit our experience or enhance it.

Here are several self-sabotaging phrases that we've heard recently. You can make your own list too, just by listening closer to what you and the people around you are saying.

1. *There's never a place to park when I need one.*
2. *Why is everything always so difficult for me?*
3. *Some things never change.*
4. *There's no possible way this is going to work out.*
5. *It's too late.*
6. *I just can't lose any weight.*

7. *It's going to be too expensive; we'll never be able to afford it.*

8. *So and so is incapable of changing; they're a lost cause.*

9. *It doesn't look very promising.*

10. *Easier said than done.*

11. *Well, I'll be damned.*

12. *It's going to be a bad allergy season this year.*

13. *I'm afraid there's not going to be a good harvest this year.*

14. *The weather is getting worse.*

15. *I'm just real sensitive to those things.*

16. *There's nothing we can do about it.*

17. *What a struggle this is.*

18. *This is a pain in the neck.*

19. *I'm getting sick and tired of all this.*

20. *The doctor says it won't go away.*

Cookies for Consciousness

We discovered a great way to stop the old habits of constantly saying unempowered words. Whenever one of our fellow Intenders caught us using "*trying*" or "*hoping*" or some self-sabotaging phrase, we would have to give them a cookie - not a store-bought cookie, but a homemade one that we'd really baked ourselves. Two things happened right away. We became better bakers, and we had all sorts of experiences that had been eluding us come into manifestation.

The Highest Light

When we first started the Intenders, it was common to hear someone putting their sick friends or family into the circle. We would talk about someone's disease, and then intend that it is healed. This practice went on for quite awhile, but we didn't seem to be getting the results we desired from it. So, one evening, we decided to ask our guides and helpers about this. The answer we received was very profound.

We were told that *when we give a name to somebody's sickness* that we are giving power unto it. We were reminded that our words have power, and when we speak the name of any disease - whether we think it is our own or someone else's - *we are actually reinforcing or feeding the disease*. This does not help us if our highest priority is to preserve and perpetuate our lives.

We were also reminded that our thoughts are things, and that we are all transmitters and receivers of thoughts. On a level which is normally invisible to us, these thoughts fly through space, just like radio or TV waves, and they are received by the person we are thinking about. When we send out a thought that pictures someone else in it, this thought is received and it tends to manifest. We are all constantly making suggestions with our thoughts to others of how we would like them to be.

So, when we envision others as suffering in any way, we are contributing to their suffering. Conversely, when we see them in their highest light - happy and full of vitality - that is the message they receive. And that is the message that will help them the most.

No one is well-served by another who, either consciously or unconsciously, talks about disease. The best thing that you can do for anyone is to hold the light for them, seeing them in their perfect state of wellness. Regardless of what they tell you about their maladies, you do them no favor by agreeing with them about their illnesses. When they are temporarily unable to hold the light for themselves, you can hold it for them. You help them by holding a vision in your mind of them in their highest light. And, in this way, you are not reinforcing their sickness and suffering. You are reinforcing their wellness.

So now, in our Intenders Circles, we refrain from naming sicknesses and diseases and, therefore, we give no power to them. We see everyone, at all times, in their highest light.

~ ~ ~ ~

Support life
Support life in every thought you have
Support life with every word you speak

Not too long ago, there was a scare that ran through the people of the Big Island of Hawaii. A group of businessmen from the mainland had decided that, in order to maintain their profits, it would be necessary to irradiate all of the papayas that were going to be shipped off of the island. The local governmental officials voted to support this endeavor and agreed to allow some nuclear materials to be brought onto the island.

It must be said that Hawaii is one of the most isolated places on the Earth, and it is cleansed constantly by the gentle tradewinds and the waves that come from across the Pacific Ocean. In the past there had never been any overriding need for radioactive products to be on the island, and a great many people did not see any reason to put the entire population and environment at risk now just so a few mainland businessmen and large-tract papaya growers could make some more money for themselves. It appeared that these business people were trying to take advantage of the Spirit of Aloha that is still a vital part of the Hawaiian way of life.

The public outcry was loud and strong. Groups hurriedly gathered together and petitions were circulated everywhere. Thousands of people spoke out in the name of the Aloha Spirit to preserve one of the cleanest environments on the Earth. All over the island, posters on storefronts and bumperstickers on cars and trucks proclaimed "I love a radiation-free Hawaii".

For several weeks, this was the main topic of discussion at our Hilo Intenders Circle. We even asked our guidance about it at the end of one of our meetings, and the answer we got was quite surprising. We were told that we might want to consider rewording the posters and bumperstickers because they weren't saying exactly what we desired them to say. Our guides said that in order for it to be possible for us to manifest a radiation-free Hawaii, we would have had to envision a radiated Hawaii first. They told us that we were subtly sabotaging ourselves when we used the word "free" in this way. For instance, they said that whenever we intend that we are stress-free or debt-free or radiation-free, we had to have first created the stress, debt or radiation in our minds. Wouldn't it be better to bypass this step by going straight to envisioning the outcome we desire from the beginning?

They said that it is very important to pay close attention to the way we phrase our words, and, in this case, the best thing that we could do for Hawaii is to always see it in its highest light.

Needless to say, we followed our guides advice that night by expressing our gratitude for our lovely island home, and by intending that Hawaii is forever pristine, beautiful, and the healthiest possible environment to raise our children and live our lives in the Spirit of Aloha.

Tony Burroughs

What if all of us were seeing everyone, including ourselves, in our highest light?

Being

The destiny of men and women on Earth today is not to be found chasing after the promise of the American Dream. Those of us who grew up in the baby boomer generation have seen the American Dream come and go. It has outlived its usefulness. There was a time when it was very attractive, but it has left many of us feeling empty. One day, we may have been at the top of the material world, enjoying all of its bounty; and, the next day, that bounty could become burdensome or nonexistent, leaving us to wonder why we spent so much time and energy pursuing it.

A common thread that runs through the minds of many of us is that there has to be more to life. There has to be something we can do, or someplace we can go, to achieve the lasting happiness that we instinctively know to be ours.

Fortunately, there is a place we can go for fulfillment that offers us a vast range of wonderful experiences. This place lies *within us* - each and every one of us. As we close our eyes and be still for a few moments, sights, sounds, and feelings that were once hidden show themselves to us. We realize that we are more than our body. We are a Being who lives inside our physical body, and this Being continues to exist long after the physical body is gone.

As we practice looking within, we find that the Spiritual Being who lives inside us is not encumbered by the manmade rules, contrived scenarios, and survival needs of the physical body. It is unlimited. It can take us to worlds we didn't previously know existed. Suddenly, we discover that the true destiny of man and woman is having free access to higher states of consciousness. We see that our future lies in other realms, other dimensions, other Universes. We feel like a seed which has remained dormant for a long time that has now popped its head above the soil, spread its new leaves out for all the world to see, and is reaching its young branches up to the sky.

Similarly, our Spiritual Being is reaching out to us offering these sublime states of joy at every moment. But before we can make contact with the Spiritual Being inside of us, we must first understand what Being means. We must become adept at the fine art of Being. Being is not doing. Being is not thinking. Being is Being. Being is sitting or lying still in any comfortable position, for any length of time, closing your eyes (unless you're already adept), but remaining alert and letting go of all of the thoughts and sensations that connect you to the physical world. In the state of Being, we cultivate stillness, always gently returning to it when it has been interrupted.

It is very helpful to practice Being everyday because Being is cumulative. It's like strengthening a muscle - the more you practice it, the better experiences you'll have. For those who persist *with the highest of intentions*, a crystal blue-white light will beckon from the darkness behind your closed eyes and angels from the heavens will sing from the depths of your silence.

Keep Moving Forward

There are times for all of us when life presents its challenges. We might feel like we've lost our way and there's nowhere to turn. Every road appears bleak, cold, unforgiving, and the voices of doubt won't give us a moment's rest.

The Intenders would like to give some encouragement to those of you who are going through your stuff. When all hope appears to be gone, your intentions are still there. Your choices are still there. Keep moving forward. Even though the voices in your head tell you that all is lost and that any further action on your part would be futile, don't give up. Remember the truth - that just because your intentions haven't manifested yet doesn't mean that they're not going to manifest.

Keep moving forward. *No matter what.* And intend that, from now on, all of your changes are gradual, gentle, and full of grace.

The Intention Process never fails. It is only when we become impatient, intolerant, or forget that our thoughts are creating our experiences that we bring suffering to ourselves. There is no situation that cannot be turned around. There is always a bright side. In every experience, there is a gift, even if we have to use a magnifying glass to find it. *We can manifest miracles as long as we never give up on our dreams, as long as we intend it and keep lining ourselves up with the highest that is within us.*

So be good to yourself. Life's experiences are meant to move us closer to realizing who we truly are. Every challenge takes us nearer to a knowing that, at our core, we are Spiritual Beings. And, always remember that things can change. Good things can happen in the blink of an eye. One moment you may be mad at the world and thinking about giving up on all that is near and dear to you - and, in the next moment, a spark of love may warm your heart and bring newfound joy into your life. Your Spirit may soar. Keep moving forward.

The Critical Point

Consider what happens when you strike a match. There is a critical point when just enough friction occurs to cause a spark to spring forth and a fire that wasn't there a moment before to burn brightly in front of you. It's the same with mankind as we move into the new millennium. It doesn't take all of us to bring about the change; it just takes enough of us to *intend* that we live in a world of peace and freedom and joy. It will happen in an instant. One moment we may still be shuffling through the shadows, and then, suddenly, in the next moment, one inspired person breaks a lifelong pattern and opens up to the highest good - and with this simple act of love, the entire human race reaches a critical point. A spark of light flickers, then bursts into flame, heralding a new standard and the life that we all deserve to live.

That person could be you.

PART IV
FREQUENTLY ASKED QUESTIONS

Q. When is the best time for an Intenders Circle?
A. Anytime. There are groups meeting on Sunday, Tuesday, and Thursday evenings in our area.

Q. What do people wear to an Intenders Circle?
A. Sometimes people are coming from work, so there's a variety of clothing. But, for the most part, we wear very comfortable clothes.

Q. What should I bring to the potluck?
A. The majority of the Intenders Circles in our area have vegetarian potlucks. Bring whatever is appropriate. (And don't forget the dessert!)

Q. Do I have to do anything special to be an Intender?
A. No. All you have to do to be an Intender of the Highest Good is tell yourself that you are one.

Q. Who can participate in Intenders Circles?
A. Everybody! We are an open group.

Q. What if someone else in the circle makes an intention that I'd also like to manifest for myself?
A. Just say "*ditto*". We say *ditto* a lot in our circles.

Q. How many Intenders can there be in a circle?
A. Most groups have found, through experience, that

up to 25 people in a circle works well. More than 25 can sometimes take a long time. (We don't like to hurry through our gratitudes and intentions.) The ideal Intenders Circle seems to be between 10 to 20 people. When a bigger crowd shows up, some groups have chosen to divide into smaller circles and go into different rooms of the house. Of course, everyone comes back together into a big circle for the toning.

Q. Can I bring my children to the Intenders?
A. Our experience has guided us to discourage people from bringing young children. Intenders meetings usually run from 2 to 3 hours, and most young children are not able to sit quietly in one place for that length of time. Some Intenders groups have a person who takes care of the children in an area that is away from the circle where the children can be told stories or play together.

Q. Can I put intentions in the circle for a friend?
A. Sure, we do it all the time. We just make sure that we include the highest good clause.

Q. The world is changing so fast for me, and I find myself getting upset when the things that I'm used to having aren't there anymore. What can I do?
A. These are the times that test your Spirit. Ordinarily, when you look closer at the situation you're in, you'll find that it isn't really so bad. It's just that you think it's bad.

If you find yourself getting upset when big changes are happening, remember to remain friendly toward others. The people around you may be the ones who'll help you. Treat them the way you'd want to be treated. Be patient, ask for what you need, and be ready to receive.

Above all, stick with the Intention Process and *keep moving forward.*

Q. It seems to me that I'll need to take some action if my intentions are going to manifest for me. Can you talk about this?

A. We've found that the recipe for successful creativity calls upon us to make use of three ingredients: Intent, Feeling, and Action. The first ingredient, *Intent*, is applied to define a desired outcome or goal. Our experience has taught us that when we make an intention, it's wise to be exact about <u>what</u> we desire to manifest, but to leave the specifics undefined when it comes to <u>how</u> or <u>when</u> our intentions will come to us. By following this guideline and invoking the highest good, we allow the Universe to utilize any one of an infinite variety of ways to bring our intention into manifestation. Intenders who cling to a single or specific route in seeking to create their abundance limit the magical workings of the Universe considerably.

The second ingredient, *Feeling*, comes into the picture in order to provide the energy needed to make our intention develop from a thought into an etheric reality that is poised and ready to blossom into the world around us. In observing many of our mighty manifesters over the years, we've come to understand that those who are able to conjure up the feeling they'll be experiencing after their goal has been reached (even though it may not have actually manifested in physical reality yet), achieve vastly better results than those who are not in touch with the power of their feelings. Said another way, if a person can maintain the feeling of gratitude in advance of the actual manifestation of their intentions, they will increase their rate of success immensely.

As our intentions begin to precipitate down from the invisible into physical manifestation, we need to be ready to apply the third ingredient: *Action*. Before taking action, however, there has to be a waiting period or pause which typically lasts a few days (although the amount of time may vary depending upon the proficiency of the manifester and whether the highest good is being served or not). This is when we let go of all attachments and concerns about our creative endeavors and retreat into a state of divine nonchalance. Taking this conscious pause allows the Universe to work at its own pace in arranging things. Then, after the waiting period is over and our intention is ready to come forth, we'll notice that a series of synchronistic "coincidences" begins to appear in our life. We will have stepped into a magical flow that is characterized by a sequence of events occuring around us that is moving us toward our desired outcome. When this flow of seemingly magical "coincidences" reveals itself, it's up to us to take the appropriate action which each synchronistic event calls for until our final goal is reached.

If, for instance, we've intended to meet our soulmate, and an attractive new person enters our life, then we would pursue that opportunity to find out if this is the love of our life, or if it is simply a contact with someone who has something else to offer us as we continue moving toward our desired relationship.

If we think we've met a potential soulmate, then we would take action to get to know this person better so we can see where the relationship leads. They may be the one who we've been longing for, or perhaps they may be someone who will introduce us to our soulmate. In either case, as opportunities like these present themselves, it's up to us to provide the appropriate action until our intention is materialized. The idea is to keep moving forward. Sometimes all we'll have to do is hold out our hand or answer the phone, but, most often, our goals are realized by following a synchronistic chain of events and opportunities, each of which leads us ever closer to "the grand finale" which is the manifestation of our original intention.

Q. You talk a lot about peace. Is peace really possible?
A. Absolutely. Once you've been *intending* for awhile, you'll look back at some of the dreams that have come true for you. You'll remember when you first decided to

make an intention to have something that you thought was almost impossible for you to have. But you took heart, said "What the heck" and went for it anyway. And then, all of a sudden - BOOMZAPWOW! - it manifested right there in front of you!

You got your first taste of the Intention Process at work, and you realized that you weren't as confined as you used to be. You could "go for it" with confidence and expect your highest intentions to come to life, no matter how difficult they appeared in the beginning. This is the attitude that will bring lasting peace to our Earth.

Everything is possible! *It starts out with a simple thought* that turns into a few spoken words, "If it be for the highest and best good, I intend that peace and love and grace return to this Earth now. So be it and so it is."

And it ends with all of us, standing in wonder, gazing out across the threshold of a new world.

PART V
What We Learned

It's been several years since this little booklet came out and during that time we learned a few things that helped make our Intenders Circle go even smoother and the Intention Process work even better. We learned, for instance, to play tag in our circle. Instead of going around the circle clockwise like we used to do, now, when an Intender is finished saying their gratitudes and intentions, they simply tag anyone anywhere else in the circle. This has done two things: first, it's more fun; and second, everyone listens closer now because the person who would have been next isn't as preoccupied thinking about what they're going to say.

We also had to adjust to the rapid growth of our Intenders Circle. When it began to get bigger, we found that it was best to write our intentions down in advance. We did this in two ways: 1.) sometimes we asked everyone to write their intentions out before they came to the meeting; and 2.) sometimes we provided people with copies of the templates on pages 70 & 71 during the potluck so they could write down their intentions then. Both of these methods have worked well for us.

Similarly, we learned to keep the potluck down to one hour or less so that our Intenders Circle doesn't go on too late into the evening. We realized that Intenders

Circles, by their very nature, are social gatherings which bring people together for a variety of reasons. Oftentimes, the sharing of food and chatting is so enjoyable that the potluck will tend to continue on indefinitely if we don't ring a bell or make an announcement that the circle is about to begin.

We also discovered that how we coach newcomers has a great impact upon how they view their experience with us. We've found that it doesn't help for us to be too picky about how they phrase their intentions. For example, the most common self-sabotaging words that newcomers use are the words *"to be."* For some reason, people tend to continue using these words in their intentions even after we've gently pointed it out to them a time or two. What we learned is that when we were too harpish about correcting the newcomers, they began to feel uncomfortable and, since it was our intention to befriend them, we turned out to be sabotaging ourselves! The solution, we found, was for us to remain patient and refrain from further coaching at that time. We stay silent, let them make a few errors, and, typically, very soon, they'll start to catch themselves before they say something that isn't going to serve them.

We recently made another change to the way we do things that has humbled us a little bit. As you can see, it says in two places in this book that *"we share our dreams instead of our dramas."* Well, nowadays that's not always the case. On evenings when the circle is smaller, we've found that it's okay to let someone who is obviously troubled by a drama to go ahead and talk about it for a few moments. Our experiences with this taught us that if we allowed them to talk openly, then we were able to help them formulate a clear intention around their drama. That way, usually within a couple of weeks, they'd come back to the circle and tell us that the intention they'd made had manifested for them and that the drama wasn't a part of their life anymore.

Every so often an Intenders Circle will attract to it a person who is totally out of sync with the rest of the group, to the point of disrupting the flow of the meetings. When this happens, someone will have to take that person aside, away from where anyone else in the circle can hear, and explain that it would be best for everyone if he or she either changes their behavior or stops coming to the circle for awhile.

This method worked for us. In our circle we had a man who started having a few drinks before he arrived, and it simply didn't work out for the rest of us. He was loud and he interrupted the person who was speaking so often that we lost the rhythm and feeling we had come to expect from our Intenders Circle. After 3 weeks of this, we took him aside and gently pointed out what he was doing and what we could achieve if he would be quiet for awhile. I thought he was going to leave and never come back, but I was pleasantly mistaken. He did leave, but he came back sober from then on and is now a bigger advocate for the Intenders than anyone. Why? Because over the next few weeks he realized that there is something special that happens when people gather under the umbrella of the highest good. He learned that an Intenders Circle is worthy of great respect in the same way one would approach something very sacred.

Darryl Lewison

Flexibility is one of the keys to having a successful Intenders Circle. We've had people who ordered our Create Your Own Community Package and have asked us what they should do next. To this we say to get a few of your like-minded friends together (it doesn't matter how many), sit in a circle, and, one at a time, start saying your gratitudes and intentions. You don't have to follow our format to the letter. Some groups don't have the potluck at all, or they have it after they've finished saying their intentions into the circle. As long as you ask for the highest good, you can do whatever is comfortable for you and your friends.

Ultimately, we've all come to understand that an Intenders Circle is designed to give us certain specific experiences. We gather together for the feeling of upliftment, to enjoy the benefits of a happy community, to manifest all sorts of things, to empower ourselves, and to come into alignment with the highest good. That's a big promise but, left to flow naturally on its own, an Intenders Circle will do all of that and more . . .

A Preview of <u>The Code</u>

We are the Intenders Tribe and you are one of us. You were with us, ages ago, when we came together and planned the Intenders Reunion. As with the 100th Monkey Principle . . . the Godspark . . . or the tipping point, the Intenders Reunion begins when enough people have let go of their old ways and opted to line up with the highest good.

The last time we met you helped us design a personal honor code which would guide your people through this time of great change and prepare you for the Reunion. We call it The Code and it contains ten intentions or "Intents" that you can set. Every time you set an Intent, you move all of us one step closer to the day of the Reunion. We have returned at this time (just as you requested) to remind you of these things so that you can get ready for the upcoming festivities.

The Reunion is at hand. The Intenders are gathering now. A place is being held in the circle for you.

We await your return . . .

The Code
Ten Intentions for a Better World

The First Intent ~ Support Life
I refrain from opposing or harming anyone. I allow others to have their own experiences. I see life in all things and honor it as if it were my own. I support life.

The Second Intent ~ Seek Truth
I follow my inner compass and discard any illusions that are no longer serving me. I go to the source. I seek truth.

The Third Intent ~ Set Your Course
I begin the creative process. I give direction to my life. I set my course.

The Fourth Intent ~ Simplify
I let go so there is room for something better to come in. I learn to trust by lining up with the highest good and knowing that I am guided, guarded, and protected at all times. I am open to receive from expected and unexpected sources. I simplify.

The Fifth Intent ~ Stay Positive
I see good, say good and do good. I accept the gifts from all of my experiences. I am living in grace and gratitude. I stay positive.

The Sixth Intent ~ Synchronize
I am in the flow, fulfilling my desires and doing what I came here to do. Allowing beauty to guide me, I step into the present where great mystery and miracles abide. I synchronize.

The Seventh Intent ~ Serve Others
I practice love in action. I always have enough to spare and enough to share. I am available to help those who need it. I serve others.

The Eighth Intent ~ Shine Your Light
I am a magnificent being, awakening to my highest potential. I express myself with joy, smiling easily and laughing often. I shine my light.

The Ninth Intent ~ Share Your Vision
I create my ideal world by envisioning it and telling others about it. I share my vision.

The Tenth Intent ~ Synergize
I see Humanity as One. I enjoy gathering with light hearted people regularly. When we come together, we set the stage for Great Oneness to reveal Itself. We synergize.

An Excerpt from
The Code
Book 1
Intentions in Action

**_The following message comes from a recent
Spiritual Guidance Session at our Intenders Circle_**

_Historically, over many hundreds of thousands
of years, beings from all across the cosmos
have come to the Earth and planted, as well as
maintained, certain thoughtforms in your world.
Some of these beings, like Jesus Christ and the
Ascended Masters, have infused your world with
thoughtforms of love, mercy, and compassion,
with the intention of helping you to achieve the
highest experience available to you, which is
to become one with God in this lifetime. Other
beings who have visited your Earth have also
seeded your world with thoughtforms, however
these have not been beneficial to you. These
beings have literally fed themselves from your
energy, like parasites or pirates, robbing you of
your precious energy and taking it for their own
selfish purposes. In order to do this, they have_

filled your etheric environment with negative thoughts which are designed to enslave you and keep you living at a low level of existence.

To extricate yourselves from these selfish influences, you must understand that you, as human beings, are infinitely powerful in your own right. Your attention is of the utmost importance, and depending upon which thoughts you choose to put your attention on, and depending upon the words you speak, you can either give full expression to your power or you can give it away. The beings who would steal your energy are very adept at their deceptive practices, however there is one vital piece of information that they have systematically withheld from you, and it is this: <u>you manifest what you say you want and you manifest what you say you don't want</u>.

This means that when you express yourself in a negative fashion, you draw the exact opposite of what you desire to yourself. An example of this is evident when you say that you don't want an accident or a sickness to occur. What most of you don't understand is that by talking about anything - whether you want it or you don't - you invoke it; you attract it into your experience.

You see people do this all the time. They'll be talking about something they wouldn't want to happen and, sure enough, it happens. What they weren't aware of is that, in their thinking processes, they pictured it happening. Since their thoughts are always creating their future, they, in fact, brought it to life when they said they didn't want it to happen.

Some thoughtforms are designed to play tricks on you, having you believe that you are keeping your undesired experiences at bay by voicing your resistance to them. Now, however, as you're beginning to explore, more closely, how your thinking works, you can see that you are undermining or sabotaging yourself by all your negative talk; that you are the cause of your calamities by the fact that you talk about them.

The antidote to having calamities and accidents befall you is to speak only in the positive, to be even more vigilant of what you're saying, and to stop yourself before you give voice to the negative. Then, you can replace the "I don't wants" and all the talk of calamities by saying what you do want. If, for instance, you catch yourself saying, "I don't want war" - which, as you have learned, will only conjure up more aggression and violence - instead, you can say, "I intend that I am living in peace." As you phrase your words like this, you invoke only the positive. There's no possibility for war because you haven't mentioned anything about it.

Integrating positive languaging into your everyday vocabulary may take a little bit of practice. As you become more aware of what you are saying, your old negative habits will tend to surface and it will be common for you to have to take a few moments to figure out the positive way to say something. This is the same as in your Intenders Circles, where you have often had to help each other find a positive way to phrase an intention. It is good that you have learned to do this because this exercise has served you to become more positive people. You've begun to look upon these instances as an opportunity to sharpen your creative abilities. While you've found that it's challenging at times to speak positively, you've also learned that it can be fun as well. That's the spirit with which we in the higher realms recommend you approach positive languaging. Make it fun.

After all, having fun is always a positive thing.

~ A Final Note ~

That which is meant to be yours will come to you. Just as those of you who are aligned with the highest good will eventually experience your highest ideal, so shall your daily needs be met. You need never worry about your survival because there was a special mechanism put into place long ago which regulates and guarantees that everything you need will be there for you in the exact moment that you need it. Oftentimes it will not appear until the instant before it is needed, but you may be assured that while you are waiting you are being strengthened. As you learn to trust in this wondrous process, the obstacles and hardships of life fall by the wayside and are replaced by a serenity that knows no limit.

These times of great upheaval are truly gifts unto you. You are constantly surrounded by an environment that is conducive for bringing out your most fulfilling form of expression. Your ego, the part of you which is in service to yourself, is giving way to a much larger, grander you - the you that is in service to others. You are blossoming in all your glory, and it is this blossoming that you have always longed for. Be open, be available, and, in the meantime, be at peace. Your prayers and intentions are all being answered.

My Gratitudes

I am grateful for my health, my family + friends + all the good people in my life. I am grateful for the prosperity + material comforts I enjoy.

My Intentions

I intend that I am joyful & happy at all times. I intend that I am in perfect health physically + mentally at all times. I intend that I am always guided guarded & pro-tected. I intend that I am at peace and on purpose, that all my thoughts, words + actions serve the highest good of the Universe.

And I make all of these intentions for the Highest Good of the Universe, myself, and everyone everywhere.   So Be It and So It Is !

HOW TO ORDER FROM US

1.) Call us tollfree at: 1-888-422-2420

2.) Visit our website at: www.intenders.com

THE INTENDERS HANDBOOK
**A Guide to the Intention Process
and the Conscious Community**
ISBN 0-9654288-1-8
$4.00 (US) + S+H

THE HIGHEST LIGHT TEACHINGS
The companion to The Intenders Handbook
ISBN 0-9654288-4-2
$4.95 (US) + S+H

THE INTENDERS OF THE HIGHEST GOOD
The Adventure Novel by Tony Burroughs
ISBN 0-9654288-0-X
$15.00 (US) + S+H

THE INTENDERS VIDEO
The Intention Process:
**A Guide for Conscious Manifestation
and Community-Making**
ISBN 0-9654288-3-4
$14.95 (US) + S+H

CREATE YOUR OWN COMMUNITY PACKAGE
10 Intenders Handbooks + 1 Intenders DVD
$39.00 (US) + S+H

THE CODE - Intentions in Action
by Tony Burroughs
$16.95 (US) + S+H

THE CODE - The Reunion: A Parable for Peace
by Tony Burroughs
$16.95 (US) + S+H